Everyday English

Book 2
Second Edition
Teacher's Manual

Barbara Zaffran
Staff Development Specialist in
ESL and Native Languages
New York City

David Krulik
Former Director
Secondary-School ESL Programs
New York City

National Textbook Company
NTC a division of *NTC Publishing Group* • Lincolnwood, Illinois USA

*To Alain, with love
and remembrance*

Cover Photo Credits: ©Brent Jones (top left);
R. Krubner/H. Armstrong Roberts (top right, bottom right); J. Swider/H. Armstrong Roberts (bottom left)

Audio Production: Phyllis Dolgin

1996 Printing

Published by National Textbook Company, a division of NTC Publishing Group.
©1991 by NTC Publishing Group, 4255 West Touhy Avenue,
Lincolnwood (Chicago), Illinois 60646-1975 U.S.A.
6 7 8 9 VP 9 8 7 6 5 4 3

Contents

Introduction

Everyday English is a carefully structured, yet flexible, four-level program that provides essential life-skills information and helps students develop the language skills they need for daily real-life situations. Books 1 and 2 are designed for beginning students of English, while Books 3 and 4 may be used at the advanced beginning level. Young adult and adult students alike will benefit from the wealth of practical information and the variety of reinforcing activities found in this series. The four books may be used independently or as a set, depending on the needs of the students and the instructor.

The activities in all four levels of *Everyday English* provide plenty of opportunities for student-student interaction, since learners become more proficient in a language by using it than by simply learning about it. Active participation is often achieved when students work in pairs or groups of four or five. In this setting, the teacher is free to circulate among the groups as a facilitator, making sure that all students are participating and practicing in English. The students thus receive a great deal of individual attention in a nonthreatening environment. The activities in the *Everyday English* program are easily adaptable to whole-group, small-group, and individualized instruction, allowing teachers the flexibility of using a variety of instructional techniques.

Suggestions for Using the Material in *Everyday English*

Illustrations After an initial discussion of a chart, map, or picture to establish basic vocabulary, students can be encouraged to generate their own dialogues made up of questions and answers about the illustration. They can work in pairs or small groups, asking and answering each other's questions. Later, the new vocabulary and concepts that often arise from students' discussions of an illustration can be explored together in a whole-class discussion. As a review activity, students can even participate in a team competition to see which team can ask and/or answer the most questions about an illustration in a given period of time.

Checking Answers For exercises in which writing is required, students can do the work individually and then compare their answers with a partner. During the comparison, students are practicing their English; for example: "What do you have for number one?" "My answer is different." "Are you sure?" and so on. The students learn from each other and participate more actively than would be possible if they had to wait to be recognized by the teacher. During a peer checking session, the instructor can circulate to look over the students' work and help resolve any disagreements between partners.

Vocabulary At the beginning level, it is generally important to introduce new vocabulary before presenting a reading passage. New words are best introduced in complete sentences, preferably using the context the students will encounter in the reading passage. Realia and pictures are very helpful for communicating the meanings of new words. Synonyms and antonyms can also be used to help students grasp the meanings of unfamiliar words. Before presenting a reading passage, complete several vocabulary activities—both oral and written—to ensure that the new vocabulary is understood.

An alternative approach is to present the reading passage and allow the students to generate their own lists of new vocabulary. They can work in pairs or small groups to find the definitions and practice using the words, or you can ask them to try defining the new words using only contextual clues. It is important to let even beginning-level students confront unfamiliar information, albeit in a controlled way, so they will learn how to apply their knowledge to the task of deciphering the unknown.

Progress Reports Before beginning a unit, you might ask the students to jot down what they know about the topic. For example, you can ask a question such as "What do you know about the calendar?" Collect the papers and save them. Use the students' notes to determine how much they know, how much language they can manipulate, and what your starting point for the unit should be. Midway through the unit, return the papers and ask the students to write what they know about the topic now as well as one or two questions they'd like to ask about the topic. Collect the papers and assess how the students are progressing. Should you review some material or move more quickly? At the end of the unit, return the papers again. Ask the students to write what they know now, plus one or two questions they'd still like to ask about the topic. You may want to extend the unit to answer these questions or assign them as extra credit for small-group research. The use of progress reports such as these helps students and instructors to measure progress in a nonthreatening manner, without the use of formal tests.

Matrix Development Another excellent student-centered activity is matrix development, which allows students to practice comparing and contrasting, note taking, and reconstructing a paragraph from their notes. A matrix for a unit about the seasons might look like this:

	Summer	Winter
clothes		
months		
weather		
activities		
trees and flowers		

At the end of the unit, pairs of students can complete the matrix together, filling in words or phrases that supply the needed information. Then provide the students with a list of introductory phrases and closing phrases and ask them to write some paragraphs based on their matrices. Each student should construct a short introductory sentence, a paragraph about summer, a paragraph about winter, a paragraph comparing the two seasons, and one or two closing sentences. As an extension activity, you could have the students create their own matrices about fall and spring.

Semantic Mapping A good way to help students generate vocabulary about a particular topic is to use semantic mapping. Write a word on the board and let the students free-associate, telling any words they think of when they see that word. Write the words on the board in random order, or let a student "secretary" do so. A semantic map based on the word *dentist* might look like this:

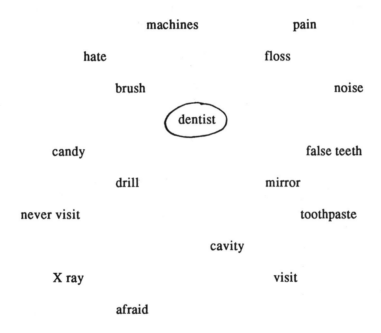

Ask the students to find the words that go together, such as:

a. afraid, pain, cavity, never go, hate
b. drill, machine, mirror, X ray, noise
c. floss, brush, toothpaste, visit
d. false teeth, cavity, candy

Have volunteers draw lines to connect the words that go together, or use different colors of chalk to circle the words in each group. Then work together to decide on category titles, such as:

a. reasons for not going to the dentist
b. dental equipment

c. ways to prevent dental problems

d. results of not visiting the dentist

To complete the activity, students can combine the words into sentences and then develop paragraphs or short compositions about the topic.

Suggestions for Use of the Cassette Tapes

Cassette tapes are available to accompany each or the four levels of the *Everyday English* program. These tapes include many of the exercises and activities found in the *Everyday English* student books and are suitable for use in the classroom or language laboratory, by groups or individuals. The cassettes provide excellent models of native English speech, making them especially valuable in situations where the teacher is not a native speaker of English or where students need exposure to voices other than that of their instructor.

The exercises that appear on the tapes are boxed with a cassette logo in the margin next to each lesson title in this manual. In order to achieve the best results from the use of the tapes instructors are encouraged to listen to the relevant sections of a tape before using the tape in class or with an individual student. In some cases, the exercise directions on the tapes are identical to those in the student books. However, the taped directions occasionally provide an alternative way to complete an exercise, placing more emphasis on aural/oral skills. For such exercises, students can later follow the written directions in their books to reinforce their work with the tape.

Everyday English provides a well-structured introduction to the English language through the use of topic-based units that present the life-skills information needed to interact and succeed in an English-speaking environment. A variety of puzzles, games, and other activities reinforce the material and enable students to feel success and note their own progress in their studies. Teachers and students alike will enjoy using this practical and yet imaginative series.

Unit 1
Time

Lesson 1
Parts of a Day

Aim: To tell time on the hour.

Materials:
- a large cardboard clock with movable hands
- a watch
- pictures or samples of an alarm clock and a clock radio

Motivation: Ask: "What time do you get up?" "What time do you go to to school?" "What time do you go to work?" "What time do you go to sleep?"

Proceedure:
a. Use a large clock, watch, or pictures of a timepiece to explain the following: face, minute hand (long hand), hour hand (short hand), second hand.
b. Show pictures of an alarm clock and a clock radio.
c. Do exercise 2 together.

Medial Summary:
a. Do exercise 3 orally.
b. Use a cardboard clock to illustrate as you teach the following: "What time is it?" "It's one o'clock." "What time is it?" "It's two o'clock." Follow this procedure for all the hours.
c. Have a student come to the front of the room and play the role of teacher as the class practices telling time on the hour.
d. Write a time on the board—for example, **1:00.** Tell the class that when the minute hand is on the 12 and the hour hand is on the 1, we say it's one **o'clock.** We can write either **1:00** or **one o'clock.**

Final Summary: Orally review everything that has been taught in this lesson. Use questions about the students' daily routines to add interest to the review.

Homework: Exercises 1, 3, and 4

Lesson 2
Telling Time: Hours and Half Hours

Aim: To tell time on the half hour.

Materials:
- a large cardboard clock with movable hands
- individual cardboard clocks for each student (If none are available, have each student make one.)

Review:
a. Go over the homework from Lesson 1.
b. Do exercises 1 through 3 of Lesson 2.
c. Review telling time on the hour with the large cardboard clock.

Motivation: Ask: "Who can write **one thirty** in numbers?"

Procedure:
a. Teach students to tell time on the half hour, using your large cardboard clock. Demonstrate:
"What time is it?" "It's one thirty."
"What time is it?" "It's two thirty."
Repeat and practice with all the half hours.
b. Review hourly and half-hourly time, using your big clock and the students' individual clocks. Have a contest to see which student sets his/her clock correctly the greatest number of times.
c. Do exercises 4 and 5 together.

Medial Summary: Set your cardboard clock for various times and ask questions such as:
"What time is it?" "It's one thirty."
"Is it two o'clock?" "No, it's one thirty."

Final Summary
a. Review the two ways of saying times on the half hour (i.e., "one thirty" or "half past one").
b. Review the meanings of A.M. and P.M.

Homework: Exercises 6 through 9

(optional)
Exercises 4,5

Lesson 3
Reading and Writing Time in Numerals

Aim: To tell time on the quarter hour.

Materials: a large cardboard clock with movable hands

Review:
a. Go over the homework from Lesson 2.
b. Practice telling time on the hour and half hour with the big clock.

Procedure: Use your big clock to demonstrate these concepts:
a. "What time is it?" "It's one fifteen."
b. "What time is it?" "It's a quarter after one."
c. "What time is it?" "It's a quarter to two."
d. "What time is it?" "It's one forty-five."

Medial Summary:
a. Do exercises 1 and 2.
b. Practice telling time on the quarter hour with your big clock.

Final Summary:
a. Review the two ways to say 1:15—"one fifteen" or "a quarter after one"—and 1:45—"one forty-five" or "a quarter to two."
b. Write the times on the board in numerals or show times on the large clock. Have individual students tell you each time in two different ways.

Homework: Exercises 3 through 6

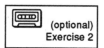
(optional)
Exercise 2

Lesson 4
Telling Time: Minutes

Aim: To read any time shown on a clock.

Materials:	a large cardboard clock with movable hands
Review:	Go over the homework from Lesson 3.
Motivation:	Do exercise 2, items *a* through *d,* orally.
Procedure:	a. Study exercise 1 together. Have students practice reading various times on your big clock.
	b. Do part *e* of exercise 2 orally.
Homework:	Exercise 2

 (optional)
Exercises 3,6

Lesson 5
Talking about Periods of Time

Aim:	To practice saying times in more than one way.
Materials:	a large cardboard clock with movable hands
Review:	Go over the homework from Lesson 4.
Motivation:	Say: "Let's see how well we can tell time."
Procedure:	a. Read exercise 1 together.
	b. Do exercise 2.
Medial Summary:	a. Demonstrate the following times on the cardboard clock: five after ten; ten after ten; ten thirty; ten thirty-five; ten forty; and so on.
	b. Practice the two ways to say various times; e.g., 9:50 = "nine fifty" or "ten minutes to ten" and 4:20 = "four twenty" or "twenty minutes after four."
Final Summary:	Do exercises 3 and 4.
Homework:	Exercises 5 through 8

 (optional)
Exercises 4,5

Lesson 6
Reading and Writing the Time in Words

Aim:	To understand and express times in words as well as in numerals.
Review:	Go over the homework from Lesson 5.
Procedure:	Do exercises 1 through 9.
Homework:	Exercise 10

Follow-Up Activities for Unit 1	1. Have the students make charts showing their daily schedules.
	2. Group the students and give each group a different train or bus schedule. Have each group make up five questions about the times on their schedule (e.g., "What time does the 1:15 train from Denver arrive in Tulsa?"). Then have the groups exchange questions and schedules, and let them answer each other's questions.

UNIT 2
The Family

 (optional)
Exercise 6

Lesson 7
Members of a Family

Aim: To learn about the family.

Materials: pictures of family members

Motivation: Ask: "Where does your family live?"
"How many people are in your family?"
Encourage: "Tell us about your family and your home."

Procedure:
a. Make a list on the board of the students' replies to the motivation questions.
b. Display pictures representing a mother, father and child. Model exercise 1 for the class while the students have their books closed. Then have the students open their books and read the exercise with you.

Medial Summary: Do exercises 2 and 3.

Final Summary:
a. Ask questions about the people in the exercise 1 picture.
b. Do exercise 4 together.

Homework: Exercises 5 and 6

(optional)
Exercise 8

Lesson 8
A Family Tree

Aim: To learn about members of the extended family.

Materials: pictures of your family members

Review:
a. Go over the homework from Lesson 7.
b. Use the pictures of your family to review the vocabulary from Lesson 7.

Motivation: Ask: "Do you know how to draw a family tree?" Discuss what a family tree is.

Procedure:
a. Do exercises 1 and 2.
b. Model exercise 3 for the class.

Medial Summary:
a. Do exercise 4.
b. Model exercise 5 for the class.
c. Teach the students that their aunt or uncle's spouse is called their uncle or aunt.
d. Ask the students about their own families, practicing the vocabulary from exercises 3 and 5.

 (optional)
Exercise 2

Lesson 9
Members of the Extended Family: My Relatives

Aim: To learn additional relationships.

Review: Go over the homework from Lesson 8.

Motivation: Encourage: "Tell us about your family."

Procedure:
a. Do exercise 1.
b. Have several pairs of students read the dialogue in exercise 2.
c. Have the students describe themselves in as many ways as they can think of (e.g., "I am my father's daughter, my aunt's niece, my brother's sister . . .").
d. Read and talk about exercise 5.

Medial Summary: Do exercise 3 orally.

Final Summary: Ask questions based on the information in exercise 5 (e.g., "Who is your spouse's sister?").

Homework: Exercises 3, 4, and 6

 (optional)
Exercise 2

Lesson 10
Review of Family Members and Relationships

Aim: To review the unit on the family.

Procedure: Have the students complete exercises 1 through 4 individually, then exchange books with a partner and check each other's work.

Homework: Exercise 5

Follow-Up Activities for Unit 2

1. Have the students make as many words as they can, using the letters in **grandfather**.
2. Teach relationships not included in this unit, such as **great-aunt** and **great-grandmother**.
3. Put a list of family members on the board (e.g., **niece, daughter, cousin, grandson**). Have the students describe each person in as many different ways as they can (e.g., "my niece is my brother's daughter, my nephew's sister, my son's cousin . . .").

UNIT 3
School

 (optional)
Exercise 1

Lesson 11
The First Day

Aim: To get to know the other students in the class.

Motivation: Ask: "What's my name?" If no one knows, tell the class your name. Then point to several students one by one and ask, "What's his/her name?"
Say: "Today we will get to know each other's names."

Procedure:
a. Read the dialogue in exercise 1. If a teacher's aide or other person is available, the two of you can play the two roles.
b. Have the students repeat each line of the dialogue after you.
c. Have small groups of students repeat each line after you. The groups can be determined by rows (or other seating arrangement) or by sex.
d. Have pairs of students role-play the dialogue for the class, changing it as appropriate to tell about themselves.

Medial Summary: Pair the students and have them do exercise 2 orally.

Final Summary: Do exercise 3 together orally.

Homework: Exercises 2 and 3

 (optional)
Exercise 2

Lesson 12
Things in the Classroom

Aim: To learn the names of objects in the classroom.

Materials: picture flashcards of the twenty objects listed in the Procedure

Review:
a. Have pairs of students role-play the dialogue from Lesson 11, changing it to describe themselves.
b. Go over the homework from Lesson 11.

Motivation: Ask the students to identify some well-known objects in your classroom, such as **pencil, table,** or **chair.** Emphasize how much the students already know.

Procedure:
a. Point to a ruler and ask: "What is this?"
Answer: "This is a ruler."
b. Use the above procedure to introduce the names of these objects:

ruler	coat hooks	table	trash can
window	chair	closet	notebook
door	book	pencil	filing cabinet
chalkboard	picture	pen	crayons
desk	eraser	chalk	lights

Stop after every five items and review. Use these suggestions:

- Straight identification: "What's this?" "It's a book."
- Erroneous identification: "Is this a desk?" "No, it's a book."
- Choice of identification: "Is this a book or a desk?" "It's a book."
- Remove an object and see if the class as a whole or an individual student can identify the missing object.
- See how many objects one student can identify.

Medial Summary: Do exercise 1 together.

Final Summary: Do exercise 2. Then review the names of the objects, using picture flashcards. Have students come to the board and write the name of the item shown on each flashcard.

Homework: Exercise 3

(optional)
Exercises 3,5

Lesson 13
People and Places in Our School

Aim: To learn about the various rooms in the school.

Materials: simplified floor plans of your school

Review:
a. Go over the homework from Lesson 12.
b. Use Total Physical Response to review the names of objects in the classroom. Give individual students commands such as "Go to the door," "Give Jonas the pen," or "Sit at my desk."

Motivation: Say: "It's important to know about our school. Let's look at this floor plan (map) and see where we go when it's time for lunch."

Procedure:
a. Continue working with the floor plan of your school.
   Ask: "Where do we go if we . . ."
   - want to find a book?
   - want to get help with a problem?
   - feel sick?
   - need paint?
   - want to hear a concert?
   - want to see a basketball game?
   - want to speak to the principal?
   - want to play soccer or football?
   - want to wash our hands?
   - want to wash our hands?
b. Go over exercise 1 together.

Medial Summary: Do exercise 2 together.

Final Summary: Do exercise 3 together. Then tour the school with the class and have the students complete exercise 4.

Homework: Exercises 5 and 6

 (optional)
Exercise 1

Lesson 14
The New Student

Aim: To learn how to get to know a new student.

Review: Go over the homework from Lesson 13.
Have several students read their dialogues and ask the class their questions. Make copies of the dialogues for use with the class later.

Motivation: Pretend that a new student is joining the class. The student has many questions:

"Where is Mr. Jones's English class?"
"Where is room 202?"
"Where is the main office?"

Ask one student to play the role of the newcomer and another student to play the role of the "old hand." Have them role-play a conversation.

Procedure: a. Read the dialogue in exercise 1 together.
b. Go over exercise 4. Discuss some possible answers with the class and then let the students write their own answers. Walk around and check their work. Ask a few students to read their dialogues to the class.

Medial Summary: Do exercise 2 together.

Final Summary: Ask comprehension questions about the dialogue. Then pair the students and have them do exercise 3 orally.

Homework: Exercises 3 and 5

 (optional)
Exercise 3

Lesson 15
Review of the School

Aim: To review the unit on the school.

Procedure: Do exercises 2 through 7 in class, varying your techniques. First do some exercises with the class as a whole. Then have one student do an exercise at the board while the other students do it in their seats. Go over the answers with the class orally, walk around and check the students' work individually, or have the students exchange books and correct each other's work. For exercises 5 and 7, let the students role-play their dialogues and ask their questions in front of the whole class or in small groups.

Homework: Exercises 1 and 8

Follow-Up Activities for Unit 3

1. Play Bingo, using the names of objects presented in this lesson.
2. Have the students make as many words as they can, using the letters in **teacher** or **basketball.**
3. Have pairs or groups of students present skits about a new student's experiences.
4. Use the dialogue in exercise 1 of Lesson 11 for a dictation activity.

UNIT 4
Money

 (optional)
Exercise 5

Lesson 16
U.S. Currency

Aim: To learn the values of U.S. coins and bills.

Materials: a sample of each coin and bill

Motivation: Ask: "How many of you have after-school or weekend jobs?" "Do you like earning money?" Encourage: "Let's learn more about American money."

Procedure:
a. Introduce the vocabulary in exercise 1:

penny	dime
nickel	quarter
change	coins
	half dollar

b. Do exercise 2 orally.

c. Study the vocabulary and pictures in exercise 3 together.

Medial Summary: Do exercise 4, using realia to demonstrate the answers if possible.

Final Summary:
a. Use TPR and your realia to review coin and bill identification.

b. Read the dialogue in exercise 5 together. Have pairs of students role-play the dialogue.

Homework: Exercises 2 and 6

 (optional)
Exercise 3

Lesson 17
Counting Money

Aim: To learn to add amounts of money.

Materials: samples of coins and bills

Review: Go over the homework from Lesson 16.

Motivation: Give one student two quarters, a dime, and a nickel. Give another student three nickels and seven pennies. Ask how much money each student has. Ask the class which student has more money.

Procedure:
a. Do exercise 1 together.

b. Have the students do exercise 2 individually and go over the answers with the class.

c. Do exercise 3 together.

Medial Summary:	Do exercise 4 orally, using realia and writing the answers on the board.
Final Summary:	a. Do exercise 5 orally.
	b. Ask the class to solve some money problems in small groups.
Homework:	Exercises 4 and 5

Lesson 18
Talking about Money

Aim:	To learn to subtract amounts of money and figure change.
Review:	a. Go over the homework from Lesson 17.
	b. Have the students do exercise 1 in small groups. Go over the possible answers as a class.
Procedure:	a. Study exercise 2 together.
	b. Read the dialogue in exercise 4 and let volunteers role-play it for the class.
Medial Summary:	Do exercise 3 on the board.
Final Summary:	Do exercise 5 orally.
Homework:	Exercises 3 and 5

Lesson 19
Review of Money

Aim:	To review the unit on money.
Review:	a. Go over the homework from Lesson 18.
	b. Use TPR and samples of coins and bills to review their their identity and value.
Procedure:	Do exercises 1 and 2 together. Try having one student read a problem from the book to another student, who writes it on the board. Then let a third student solve the problem.
Homework:	Exercises 3 and 4
Follow-Up Activities for Unit 4	1. Have the students investigate whose picture is on each coin and bill. Discuss why each person might have been chosen for this honor.
	2. Set up a "store" or a "rummage sale" in your classroom. Have students buy items from the "cashier," who must give them the correct change. Use play money and let the students price the items.

UNIT 5
Transportation

(optional)
Exercise 1

Lesson 20
Methods of Transportation

Aim: To learn about various methods of transportation.

Materials: pictures and/or models of various modes of transportation

Motivation: Ask personal question, such as: "How did you come to the United Sates?" "How do you get to school?" "In how many ways have you traveled?"

Procedure:
a. Display pictures or models of a train, boat, bus, car, airplane, truck, motorcycle, taxi, bicycle, and helicopter. Teach the names of these items and use TPR to reinforce the vocabulary.

b. Have the students do exercise1 and exchange books to check the answers.

c. Do exercise 4 together. First, establish that a boat travels on water, a plane and a helicopter travel in the air, and all the other vehicles mentioned in this lesson travel on land. Establish that ships and planes take us to places far away from our present location. All other vehicles can take us to places that are both near and far. (There are exceptions, of course, such as short rides on private planes and boats—fishing boats, sailboats, etc.—for recreational purposes.)

d. Study exercise 5 together.

Medial Summary:
a. Ask: "Who can name ten methods of transportation?"

b. Hide one of your models or pictures and have the class guess which one is missing. The first student who guesses correctly gets to hide the next item.

c. Do exercise 6 together.

Final Summary:
a. Review all ten methods of transportation, using these techniques:
   - Have a student name all the pictures/models.
   - Hold up a flashcard and have the students identify the item as quickly as they can.
   - Have the students race to unscramble words you write on the board.

b. Do exercises 7 and 9.

Homework: Exercises 2, 3, 8, and 10

(optional)
Exercise 3

Lesson 21
Traveling by Air

Aim: To learn about buying a plane ticket and taking a flight.

Materials: a map of the United States

Review:	Go over the homework from Lesson 20.
Motivation:	Display your map of the United States and ask: "Where would you like to go in the U.S.A?" After at least some of the students have volunteered a reply, discuss the different ways you could travel to those destinations. Have individuals come up to the map to illustrate the best routes.
Procedure:	a. Read the dialogue in exercise 3 and discuss the following vocabulary:

one way	to check baggage	a check
flight	round trip	takeoff
fare	to book	to board

Let pairs of students role-play the dialogue, changing it to describe trips they would like to take.

b. Do exercise 2 together.

Medial Summary:	Have the students work in groups to do exercise 1. Then make a master list together on the board.
Final Summary:	Do exercise 4 and 5 together.
Homework:	Exercises 6 and 7

(optional)
Exercises 2,3

Lesson 22
Traveling by Bus

Aim:	To learn about bus stations and traveling by bus.
Review:	Go over the homework from Lesson 21.
Motivation:	Ask: "Who has been on a bus?" "Where did you go by bus?"
Procedure:	a. Discuss the picture in exercise 2 and introduce this vocabulary:

waiting room	porter
boarding	ticket window
suitcases	

b. Do exercise 1. Then see if the students can use each word in a sentence.

c. Read and discuss the story in exercise 2.

Medial Summary:	Do exercise 3 orally.
Final Summary:	Have the students do exercise 4. Then read the story out loud so they can check their work.
Homework:	Exercises 3 and 5

(optional)
Exercise 1

Lesson 23
Traffic Signs and Rules

Aim: To learn about traffic safety signs and rules.

Materials:
- pictures or models of traffic safety signs
- pictures illustrating a traffic ticket, a pedestrian, a fire hydrant, a driveway, and the concept of **right-of-way.**

Review: Go over the homework from Lesson 22. Let pairs of students role-play the dialogues they wrote for exercise 5. Make some copies of their dialogues for future use.

Motivation: Ask: "How many of you drive?" "How many of you want to learn how to drive?" "What must you know before you can drive?"

Procedure:
a. Ask: "Where do you see traffic signs?" Elicit the answer: "On streets and highways."
b. Do exercise 1, discussing new vocabulary.
c. Tell the students that if they see a policeman directing traffic, they should obey **him,** not the traffic signs at that intersection.
d. Use pictures to explain the meanings of these words:

  pedestrian
  ticket
  fire hydrant
  right-of-way
  driveway

e. Study exercise 3 together.

Medial Summary: Do exercises 2 and 4.

Final Summary: Do exercise 5 together, discussing each situation. Do exercise 6 orally.

Homework: Exercises 6 and 7

(optional)
Exercise 3

Lesson 24
Review of Transportation

Aim: To review the unit on transportation.

Review:
a. Go over the homework from Lesson 23.
b. Use TPR and your pictures or models of traffic signs to review their identity and meaning.

Procedure:
a. Pair the students and let them ask each other the questions in exercise 1. Then have them write their own answers in their books.
b. Do exercises 2 and 3. Write the words in exercise 2 on flashcards and give ten students the cards. See how quickly they can pair themselves according to their words.
c. Have the students complete exercise 4. Let pairs of volunteers role-play their dialogues for the class.

Homework: Exercises 5, 6, 7, and 8

Follow-Up Activities for Unit 5

1. Have a "transportation hunt." Divide the class into teams and give each team a list of questions, such as:
   - Name four airports anywhere in the world.
   - Name two tunnels.
   - Name four bridges.
   - What is the speed limit on the street in front of your school?
   - How long does it take to fly from New York City to Los Angeles, California?
   - What important papers must you always have with you when you drive your car?

   Have the students work in the school library to find the answers, and award a prize to the first team to correctly answer all the questions. **Or,** assign the questions as a group homework project. The next day, you can award prizes to **all** the teams that have correctly answered the questions.

2. Have each student plan a trip, using free brochures you bring in from travel agencies and bus, plane, and train schedules. The students must write itineraries showing where, when, and how they will travel and where they will stay. Let the students describe their plans to the class.

UNIT 6
Looking for an Apartment

 (optional)
Exercise 1

Lesson 25
Kinds of Dwellings

Aim: To learn about different kinds of dwellings and how to find a place to live.

Materials:
- newspaper real estate section
- pictures of vocabulary to be taught

Motivation: Ask: "Where do you live?" "Do you live near the school or far from the school?"
"Are there many families living where you live, or does only your family live there?"
"Do you live in an apartment building or a private house?"

Procedure:
a. Introduce the folowing vocabulary, using your own picture cards and the pictures in exercise 1.

apartment building	room
private house	air conditioning
duplex	basement
apartment complex	walk-up
elevator	landlady
lease	landlord
rent	dwelling
appliances	floor

b. Do exercise 1 together, then have the students use each word in a sentence.

c. Ask: "Where do we look for an apartment or a private house?" Look at the newspaper real estate section and read several classified ads together. Discuss what kind of dwellings would be preferable for your students. Remind them that they must take several factors into consideration, among them: size, appliances or connections available, cost, location, age of the building, and restrictions (for example, no pets or children allowed).

d. Do exercise 2 together.

Medial Summary:
a. Explain these abbreviations to the class:

rm.	trans.
apt.	shopg.
bdrm.	$350/mo.
avail.	betw.
nr.	spk.

b. Read the ad in exercise 3 together. Then have the students answer the questions in exercise 3.

Final Summary: Do exercise 4 and 6 together.

Homework: Exercises 5 and 7

(optional)
Exercise 1

Lesson 26
Rooms in Homes

Aim: To learn about the different rooms in an apartment or house.

Materials: pictures of the various rooms in a home

Review: Go over the homework from Lesson 25.

Motivation: Ask: "What kinds of rooms can you find in an apartment or a house?"

Procedure: a. display pictures of these rooms and introduce the new vocabulary:

bedroom	dining room
living room	garage
bathroom	attic
kitchen	basement
den	nursery

   b. Do exercise 1. Tell the class that all of these rooms can be found in both apartments and houses except a basement and an attic. Those rooms are usually found only in a private house.

   c. Discuss what each room is for. Read exercise 2 together.

Medial Summary: Do exercise 3 together.

Final Summary: a. Review the names of the rooms, asking the students questions such as "Where do you sleep?" or "Where does your family eat?" Be sensitive to cultural and economic differences that may affect the answers.

   b. Do exercise 4.

Homework: Exercises 5, 6, and 7

(optional)
Exercise 4

Lesson 27
Home Furnishings

Aim: To learn about objects in the kitchen and bathroom.

Materials: • samples or pictures of household items
   • pictures of the rooms in an apartment or house

Review: a. Go over the homework from Lesson 26.
   b. Use TPR and your pictures to review the names of the rooms in a house.

Motivation: Ask: "Where do we eat?" "How many things can you name in the kitchen?"

Procedure: a. List the students' replies to the above questions on the board.
   b. Teach the new kitchen vocabulary:

stove	refrigerator
oven	cabinets
sink	dishwasher

c. Do exercise 1 orally and study exercise 2 together.

d. Ask: "Where do we wash up?" "How many things can you name in the bathroom?" Write the students' answers on the board.

e. Teach the new bathroom vocabulary:

sink	bath mat
shower	towel rack
bathtub	mirror
toilet	hamper
medicine cabinet	tile
shower curtain	

f. Do exercise 4 orally and study exercise 5 together.

Medial Summary: Do exercises 3 and 6.

Final Summary: Do exercises 7 and 8.

Homework: Exercises 1, 4, and 9

 (optional)
Exercise 1

Lesson 28
More Home Furnishings

Aim: To learn about objects in the living room and bedroom.

Materials:
- samples or pictures of household items
- pictures of the rooms in an apartment or house

Review: Go over the homework from Lesson 27.

Motivation: Ask: "Where do we entertain visitors or sit down to relax?" "Where do we sleep?" "How many things can you name that are found in these rooms?"

Procedure:
a. List the students' replies to the above questions on the board.

b. Teach the new living-room vocabulary:

couch (sofa)	venetian blinds
armchair	curtains
rug	lamp
carpeting	breakfront
bookcase	end table
coffee table	

c. Do exercise 1 orally and study exercise 2 together.

d. Teach the new bedroom vocabulary:

bed	dresser
nightstand	dressing table
clothes closet	

e. Do exercise 4 orally and study exercise 5 together.

f. Teach vocabulary that is applicable for all rooms, such as:

shades	lamp	pictures
radiator	mirror	plants
curtains (drapes)	trash can	ceiling
floor	wall	door
window	venetian blinds	rug

Final Summary: Do exercises 8 and 9.

Homework: Exercises 1, 4, and 7

(optional)
Exercise 5

Lesson 29
Housewares

Aim: To learn about objects used in cleaning, eating, and preparing food.

Materials: samples or pictures of household items

Review: Go over the homework from Lesson 28.

Motivation: Ask: "Where do we entertain?" "Where do we eat?" "What items do we use in these rooms?"

Procedure:
a. List the students' replies to the above questions on the board.
b. Do exercise 1.
c. Teach the new kitchen vocabulary:

salt and pepper shakers	knife (knives)	can opener
cups	broom closet	microwave oven
glasses	vacuum cleaner	sponge
pots	saucers	mop
pans	blender	napkins
dishes	toaster	spoons
silverware	forks	

d. Do exercise 2.

Medial Summary: Do exercise 3.

Final Summary: Have the students do exercise 4. Let volunteers read their paragraphs to the class.

Homework: Exercises 5 and 6

(optional)
Exercise 5

Lesson 30
More Housewares

Aim: To learn about objects used in the bedroom and laundry room.

Materials: samples or pictures of household items

Review: Go over the homework from Lesson 29.

Motivation: Ask: "Where do we sleep?" "Where do we wash our clothes?" "What items do we use in these rooms?"

Procedure: a. List the students' replies to the above questions on the board.

b. Teach the new bedroom vocabulary:

sheet	pillowcase
blanket	pillow
clock radio	alarm clock

c. Do exercises 1 and 2.

d. Teach the new laundry-room vocabulary:

clothesline
hamper
laundry detergent
washing machine
dryer

e. Do exercises 4 and 5.

Medial Summary: Do exercises 3 and 6.

Final Summary: Do exercise 7.

Homework: Exercise 8

(optional)
Exercise 2

Lesson 31
Rental Advertisements

Aim: To learn the procedure for finding and renting an apartment.

Review: Go over the homework from Lesson 30.

Procedure: a. Do exercise 1 orally.

b. Read exercise 2 together and then let pairs of students role-play the dialogue for the class.

c. Have the students do exercise 3 individually. Pair them and let the partners ask each other their questions.

Homework: Exercises 1 and 4

(optional)
Exercise 3

Lesson 32
Review of Rooms and Furnishings

Aim: To review the unit on homes and their contents.

Review: Go over the homework from Lesson 31.

Procedure: Complete exercises 1–7 in class. Use varying techniques, allowing students to work individually, in pairs, and in small groups.

Homework: Exercises 8–11

1. Play the game "Where Am I?" Describe a room and let the students guess what room you're in. The first student to guess correctly gets to describe the next room.

2. Have the students make as many words as they can, using the letters in **breakfront.**

3. Play the game "Twenty Questions." Write the names of pieces of furniture and other household objects on small slips of paper and put them in a bag. Let one student at a time draw a slip from the bag. The rest of the class must ask **yes/no** questions until they guess the object or reach a total of twenty questions. (Examples of questions: "Is it in the bedroom?" "Is it on the wall?" "Do we cook in it?" "Does it have drawers?" "Is it an alarm clock?")

UNIT 7
Careers

 (optional)
Exercises 2,5

Lesson 33
Some Occupations

Aim: To become familiar with various careers.

Materials: flashcards with pictures of various careers.

Motivation: Ask: "What do you want to do when you finish school?" "What kinds of work do some of your relatives and family friends do?"

Procedure:
a. List the students' replies to the above questions on the board and briefly discuss each career that is mentioned.
b. Do exercise 1.
c. Study exercises 2 and 5 together.

Medial Summary: Do exercises 3 and 4 orally.

Final Summary:
a. Play a team identification game with your career flashcards.
b. Do exercise 6 together.

Homework: Exercises 3, 4, and 7

 (optional)
Exercises 1,3

Lesson 34
What Workers Do on the Job

Aim: To learn about more careers.

Materials: flashcards with pictures of various careers

Review: Go over the homework from Lesson 33.

Motivation: Ask: "What are some other careers you know something about—or would like to know something about?"

Procedure: Study exercises 1 and 3 together.

Medial Summary:
a. Play "Who am I?" One student describes a career and the class must guess which career he/she is describing. The first student to guess correctly gets to describe the next career.
b. Do exercise 2.

Final Summary:
a. Play a team game, using your career flashcards. The team that correctly identifies the most careers wins.
b. Do exercise 4.

Homework: Exercise 5

(optional)
Exercise 2

Lesson 35
More Occupations

Aim: To discuss additional careers and review those already presented.

Review: Go over the homework from Lesson 34.

Motivation: Have the students report orally on one of the two careers they wrote about in their homework.

Procedure: a. Play Bingo as described in exercise 1.

b. Complete exercise 3 together, briefly discussing each career listed.

c. If your students show special interest in any of these careers, you might obtain films on those careers or on the working world in general. Also, consider asking some of the students' parents to come to class and tell about their work and why they chose it.

d. For further review, have the class play "Twenty Questions." Students ask the leader **yes/no** questions about a mystery career. They must guess the career in twenty or fewer questions. The first student who guesses correctly becomes the next leader.

Homework: Exercise 2

(optional)
Exercise 5

Lesson 36
Seeking Employment

Aim: To learn how to look for a job.

Materials: • the want-ad section of a local newspaper
• sample résumés

Review: a. Go over the homework from Lesson 35.

b. Conduct a flashcard review of all the careers learned so far.

Motivation: Say: "Today we're going to look for a job." Show the want ads and continue: "First let's learn some vocabulary, and then we'll read some ads."

Procedure: a. Introduce the vocabulary in exercise 1:

full-time job	temporary job
part-time job	permanent job
interview	employment agency
cancel	résumé
postpone	

Then read exercise 1 together.

b. Read several ads with the class and determine if the jobs are part-time, full-time, permanent, temporary, and so on. Explain what the abbreviations stand for.

c. Show your sample résumés and talk about the function of a résumé. Discuss the kinds of information a résumé should include. Have the students do exercise 3.

Final Summary: a. Pass out copies of want ads (newspaper pages or Xeroxed sheets). Ask the students to read several ads on their own and choose three jobs they would like to have.

b. Do exercises 4 and 6.

Homework: Exercise 5

(optional)
Exercise 1

Lesson 37
Job Interviews

Aim: To learn what to do and say in a job interview.

Review: Go over the homework from Lesson 36.

Motivation: Say: "Let's practice what to do and say during a job interview."

Procedure: a. Read the dialogue in exercise 1. Discuss Helena's answers to the interviewer's questions. Are they good answers? Let pairs of students role-play the dialogue.

b. Do exercise 2 together orally.

c. Discuss the importance of looking neat and being on time for a job interview. Also talk about showing interest and respect and answering questions honestly but in a way that emphasizes your strengths.

Homework: Exercise 2

(optional)
Exercise 2

Lesson 38
Review of Careers

Aim: To review the unit on careers.

Review: Go over the homework from Lesson 37.

Procedure: Do exercises 1–5 in class. Use varying techniques, allowing students to work individually, in pairs, and in small groups.

Homework: Exercises 6, 7, and 8

Follow-Up Activities for Unit 7

1. Have the students make as many words as they can, using the letters in **real estate agent**.
2. Have each student interview someone about his/her job and then make an oral report to the class.
3. If any of your students have part-time jobs, let them come to school dressed as if for work and tell the class about what they do at work.
4. Invite a representative from a local college or business to come in and discuss the education, training, and other qualifications needed for various careers.

Answer Key

If the answers to an exercise are not provided here, those answers are either very basic or may vary from student to student. The page numbers shown here are those of the student book.

UNIT 1   **Time**

Lesson 1:   Parts of a Day
Exercise 3   (Page 2)   1. minute hand   2. hour hand   3. alarm clock   4. clock radio

Lesson 2:   Telling Time: Hours and Half Hours
Exercise 5   (Page 4)   1. a   2. b   3. b   4. a   5. b

Lesson 6:   Reading and Writing the Time in Words
Exercise 10   (Page 17)
ACROSS: 1. 1:45   3. 6:55   6. 3:10   7. 10:30   8. 6:25   13. 9:02   14. 1:38
16. 5:45   17. 4:00   18. 12:00
DOWN: 1. 1:56   2. 5:35   3. 6:05   4. 5:15   5. 5:35   9. 2:39   10. 12:50
11. 11:50   12. 10:00   15. 8:40

UNIT 2:   **The Family**

Lesson 7:   Members of a Family
Exercise 5   (Page 19)   1. brother   2. parent   3. children   4. father   5. mother
6. sister   7. child   8. son   9. daughter   10. baby

Lesson 8:   A Family Tree
Exercise 4   (Page 22)   1. grandparents   2. grandchildren   3. grandson   4. granddaughter
5. grandfather   6. grandfather   7. grandmother   8. grandmother   9. brothers
10. sister
Exercise 6   (Page 22)   1. b   2. h   3. a   4. f   5. g   6. c   7. e   8. d
Exercise 8   (Page 23)   1. b   2. c   3. b   4. a   5. a

Lesson 9:   Members of the Extended Family: My Relatives
Exercise 6   (Page 27)   1. c   2. d   3. a   4. e   5. b

Lesson 10:   Review of Family Members and Relationships
Exercise 1   (Page 27)   1. True   2. False   3. True   4. True   5. False
Exercise 2   (Page 28)   1. uncle   2. mother-in-law   3. aunt   4. niece   5. sister-in-law
6. grandmother   7. cousin   8. cousin   9. uncle   10. brother-in-law   11. stepsister
12. father-in-law
Exercise 3   (Page 28)
Mystery words: family trees

Exercise 4 (Page 29) 1. husband 2. sister 3. mother 4. parent 5. uncle
Mystery word: house
Exercise 5 (Page 29)
ACROSS: 1. grandfather 4. in-law 6. son 7. nephew 10. niece 13. daughter
14. mom 16. husband 20. he 21. cousins 23. dish 24. hill 26. boy
28. parents 29. sister
DOWN: 1. grandmother 2. niece 3. aunt 4. in 5. law 6. spouse 8. papa
9. wed 11. children 12. brother 15. mother's 17. uncle 18. blue 19. noise
22. soap 25. girl 26. be 27. or

UNIT 3:   **School**

Lesson 12:   Things in the Classroom
Exercise 2 (Page 32) 1. desk (picture e) 2. door (c) 3. pen (n) 4. trash can (p)
5. eraser (j) 6. chair (g) 7. coat hooks (k) 8. window (b) 9. notebook (q)
10. chalkboard (d) 11. pencil (m) 12. crayons (r) 13. closet (l) 14. filing
cabinet (h) 15. chalk (o) 16. table (f) 17. lights (t) 18. book (s) 19. pictures (i)
20. ruler (a)

Lesson 14:   The New Student
Exercise 2 (Page 37) 1. new girl 2. name 3. very nice 4. a good student
5. is she 6. China 7. years old 8. class 9. see her 10. I did
Exercise 5 (Page 39)
Mystery word: principal

Lesson 15:   Review of the School
Exercise 2 (Page 40) 1. door 2. pen 3. chalk 4. light 5. notebook
6. trash can 7. table 8. ruler 9. pencil 10. filing cabinet
Exercise 4 (Page 41) 1. False 2. False 3. False 4. True 5. True 6. False
7. True 8. True 9. False 10. True
Exercise 6 (Page 43) 1. window 2. door 3. table 4. chair 5. chalk
6. lights 7. closet 8. ruler 9. wall 10. nurse
Exercise 8 (Page 44)
ACROSS: 1. library 3. chairs 5. student 8. week 9. etc. 10. books
13. teachers 16. tall 19. tie 21. make 23. did 24. notebook 28. erase
30. office 31. walls
DOWN: 2. auditorium 3. chalk 4. ruler 5. school 6. table 7. light 11. speak
12. type 14. cafeteria 15. sit 17. loud 18. pencils 20. ink 22. door
23. draft 25. ball 26. pen 27. new 28. ex 29. art

UNIT 4:   **Money**

Lesson 16:   U.S. Currency
Exercise 2 (Page 45) 1. b 2. c 3. a 4. d 5. f 6. e
Exercise 4 (Page 46) 1. dimes 2. pennies 3. quarters 4. nickels

Lesson 17:   Counting Money
Exercise 1 (Page 48) 1. b 2. b 3. a 4. c 5. c

Lesson 18: Talking about Money

Exercise 3 (Page 52) 1. 19¢ 2. 1¢ 3. 15¢ 4. 10¢ 5. 18¢ 6. 5¢ 7. 71¢ 8. 10¢ 9. 12¢ 10. $3.70

Lesson 19: Review of Money

Exercise 1 (Page 53) 1. $1.35 2. $1.04 3. $10.50 4. $1.10 5. $6.00

Exercise 2 (Page 54) 1. 6¢ 2. 20¢ 3. 9¢ 4. 21¢ 5. 0

Exercise 3 (Page 54) 1. nickel 2. dollar 3. dime 4. penny

Exercise 4 (Page 54) 1. dime 2. dollar 3. penny 4. nickel 5. change

Mystery word: money

UNIT 5: **Transportation**

Lesson 20: Methods of Transportation

Exercise 1 (Page 55) 1. airplane 2. car 3. train 4. taxi 5. boat 6. bicycle 7. bus 8. truck 9. helicopter 10. motorcycle

Exercise 2 (Page 56) 1. airplane 2. car 3. truck 4. boat 5. bicycle

Mystery word: train

Exercise 3 (Page 56) 1. train 2. boat 3. bus 4. car 5. helicopter 6. taxi 7. airplane 8. truck 9. motorcycle 10. bicycle

Exercise 4 (Page 57) 1. bicycle, car, bus, taxi 2. airplane, boat 3. airplane, bus, car, train 4. car, bus, motorcycle, taxi, truck

Exercise 7 (Page 59) 1. c 2. a 3. b 4. e 5. d

Exercise 8 (Page 60) 1. plane 2. taxi 3. boat 4. ship 5. train 6. truck 7. bridge 8. route 9. ocean 10. water

Lesson 21: Traveling by Air

Exercise 2 (Page 62) 1. h 2. d 3. j 4. a 5. g 6. b 7. i 8. c 9. f 10. e

Exercise 4 (Page 63) 1. plane ticket 2. round-trip 3. tourist 4. takeoff 5. one hour

Exercise 6 (Page 64) 2, 4, 1, 3, 5

Exercise 7 (Page 64) 1. luggage 2. check 3. round-trip 4. suitcase 5. baggage 6. fare

Mystery word: flight

Lesson 22: Traveling by Bus

Exercise 1 (Page 65) 1. d 2. a 3. e 4. b 5. c

Lesson 23: Traffic Signs and Rules

Exercise 6 (Page 70) 1. d 2. a 3. e 4. c 5. b

Lesson 24: Review of Transportation

Exercise 2 (Page 72) 1. d 2. h 3. f 4. g 5. a 6. e 7. i 8. j 9. c 10. b

Exercise 3 (Page 72) 1. F 2. T 3. F 4. T 5. F 6. F 7. T 8. T 9. T 10. F

Exercise 5 (Page 73)   1. road   2. plane   3. traffic   4. detour   5. bridge
6. fare   7. no parking   8. round-trip   9. one-way   10. stop   11. boarding
12. train   13. exit   14. take off
Mystery word: transportation
Exercise 6 (Page 74)
ACROSS: 1. one-way   4. traffic   8. filled   10. sit   11. pen   12. detour
14. red   16. parking   17. road   20. way   22. auto   23. waste   24. ride
25. green   26. sun   27. pedestrians
DOWN: 2. exit   3. yield   5. railroad   6. fare   7. car   8. fire hydrants   9. stop
11. park   13. right-of-   15. driver   18. dead-end   19. lane   21. right
Exercise 8 (Page 75)
Mystery word: motorcycle

UNIT 6: **Looking for an Apartment**

Lesson 25: Kinds of Dwellings
Exercise 1 (Page 76)   1. apartment building (picture j)   2. private house (e)
3. duplex (h)   4. apartment complex (o)   5. elevator (a)   6. rooms (c)   7. appliances (l)
8. air conditioning (n)   9. basement (b)   10. walk-up (d)   11. lease (f)   12. rent (g)
13. advertisement (i)   14. dwellings (k)   15. floor (m)
Exercise 5 (Page 79)   1. a   2. b   3. b   4. a   5. a   6. b   7. b   8. b   9. a
10. b

Lesson 26: Rooms in Homes
Exercise 1 (Page 82)   1. bedroom (picture f)   2. living room (e)   3. bathroom (b)
4. kitchen (j)   5. den (g)   6. dining room (i)   7. attic (c)   8. basement (h)
9. garage (d)   10. nursery (a)
Exercise 3 (Page 83)   1. h   2. g   3. b   4. j   5. a   6. i   7. c   8. f   9. e
10. d
Exercise 5 (Page 84)   1. living room   2. bathroom   3. bedroom   4. basement
5. den
Mystery word: lease

Lesson 27: Home Furnishings
Exercise 1 (Page 86)   1. stove   2. sink   3. refrigerator   4. kitchen cabinets
5. dishwasher
This room is a **kitchen.**
Exercise 3 (Page 86)   1. d   2. a   3. e   4. c   5. b
Exercise 4 (Page 87)   1. sink   2. shower   3. bathtub   4. toilet   5. bath mat
6. mirror   7. medicine cabinet   8. shower curtain   9. tile   10. towel rack
This room is a **bathroom.**
Exercise 6 (Page 87)   1. e   2. g   3. d   4. f   5. h   6. c   7. b   8. a

Lesson 28: More Home Furnishings
Exercise 1 (Page 90)   1. breakfront   2. end table   3. couch (sofa)   4. armchair
5. rug   6. carpeting   7. bookcase   8. venetian blinds   9. curtains   10. lamp
11. shade   12. coffee table
This room is a **living room.**

Exercise 3 (Page 91) 1. d 2. g 3. j 4. b 5. i 6. e 7. h 8. f 9. a 10. c

Exercise 4 (Page 91) 1. bed 2. nightstand 3. dresser 4. dressing table
5. clothes closet

This room is a **bedroom.**

Exercise 6 (Page 92) 1. c 2. e 3. a 4. d 5. b

Lesson 29: Housewares

Exercise 3 (Page 94) 1. cup 2. glass 3. saucer 4. blender 5. toaster
6. pots 7. pan 8. plates 9. silverware 10. fork 11. knife 12. spoon
13. pitcher 14. vacuum cleaner 15. can opener 16. microwave oven 17. sponge
18. mop 19. napkins 20. salt and pepper shakers

Exercise 5 (Page 95) 1. F 2. F 3. T 4. T 5. F

Lesson 30: More Housewares

Exercise 2 (Page 96) 1. sheet 2. pillow (or pillowcase) 3. blanket 4. alarm
clock 5. clock radio

Exercise 3 (Page 96) 1. e 2. a 3. d 4. b 5. c

Exercise 5 (Page 97) 1. clothesline 2. laundry detergent 3. hamper
4. washing machine 5. dryer

Exercise 6 (Page 97) 1. d 2. a 3. b 4. e 5. c

Exercise 7 (Page 97) 1. F 2. T 3. T 4. F 5. F 6. F 7. T 8. F

Lesson 32: Review of Rooms and Furnishings

Exercise 1 (Page 100) 1. couch (or sofa) 2. chair 3. table 4. bed 5. dresser
6. breakfront 7. bookcase 8. armchair 9. end table 10. nightstand

Exercise 2 (Page 101) 1. lamp (picture c) 2. sink (l) 3. stove (d) 4. refrigerator (m)
5. bathtub (h) 6. toilet (k) 7. rug (s) 8. curtains (p) 9. trash can (n) 10. medicine
cabinet (f) 11. pictures (j) 12. pot (a) 13. pan (r) 14. towels (g) 15. silverware (o)
16. vacuum (i) 17. pillow (b) 18. blender (q) 19. blanket (t) 20. hamper (e)

Exercise 5 (Page 102) 1. c 2. e 3. a 4. g 5. i 6. b 7. h 8. d 9. f

Exercise 6 (Page 103) 1. refrigerator, kitchen 2. couch (or sofa), living room
3. lamp, nightstand, bedroom 4. armchair, living room 5. bed, bedroom
6. medicine cabinet, bathroom 7. toilet, bathroom
8. washing machine, laundry room 9. coffee table, living room 10. stove, kitchen

Exercise 7 (Page 104) 1. roof 2. closet 3. stairs 4. living room 5. kitchen
6. bedroom 7. walls 8. dining room 9. window 10. elevator 11. garage
12. door 13. bathroom 14. floor 15. nursery 16. ceiling 17. carpeting
18. chimney 19. fire escape 20. balcony

Exercise 8 (Page 105) 1. dresser 2. sheet 3. blanket

Mystery word: bed

1. cook 2. stove 3. refrigerator 4. cabinets

Mystery word: sink

Exercise 9 (Page 106)

Mystery word: roof

Exercise 10 (Page 106)

ACROSS: 1. shower 3. refrigerator 9. man 11. garbage 12. bed 14. dressers

17. table 18. silverware 20. pot 21. plan 22. not 25. gas 26. glass
29. pillowcases 30. vacuums 31. am 32. bedroom
DOWN: 1. shades 2. robe 3. rugs 4. fork 5. elevators 6. am 7. tablecloths
8. one 10. ceiling 13. dining room 15. sheets 16. broom 17. to 19. walk-ups
20. pillow 23. oat 24. stove 27. blue 28. ice 31. at
Exercise 11 (Page 107) 1. sheets 2. drain 3. clock 4. lamp 5. plants
6. wall 7. floor 8. table 9. sink 10. closet

UNIT 7:   **Careers**

Lesson 33:   Some Occupations
Exercise 4 (Page 109) 1. T 2. F 3. F 4. T 5. T
Exercise 6 (Page 110) 1. g or c 2. d 3. i 4. a 5. j 6. h 7. e 8. b
9. f 10. c or g
Exercise 7 (Page 110) 1. baker 2. waitress 3. butcher 4. principal 5. artist
6. doctor 7. pilot 8. plumber 9. judge 10. mechanic

Lesson 34:   What Workers Do on the Job
Exercise 4 (Page 112) 1. doctor 2. barber 3. composer 4. farmer 5. dentist
6. architect 7. travel agent 8. accountants 9. actors 10. secretary 11. baker
12. pilot 13. mechanic 14. actor 15. loader 16. racer 17. engineer 18. jobs
Mystery word: electricians

Lesson 35:   More Occupations
Exercise 2 (Page 114) 1. homemaker 2. teacher 3. plumber 4. author
5. principal 6. lawyer 7. police officer 8. farmer 9. dentist 10. accountant

Lesson 36:   Seeking Employment
Exercise 2 (Page 116) 1. j 2. g 3. b 4. h 5. f 6. i 7. c 8. d 9. a
10. e
Exercise 4 (Page 118) 1. F 2. T 3. F 4. F 5. T
Exercise 6 (Page 119) 1. artist 2. doctor 3. dentist 4. musician 5. mechanic

Lesson 38:   Review of Careers
Exercise 3 (Page 122) 1. b 2. i 3. j 4. a 5. c 6. h 7. f 8. d 9. e
10. g
Exercise 6 (Page 123) 1. pilot 2. lawyer 3. musician 4. mechanic 5. butcher
6. teacher 7. architect
Mystery word: plumber
Exercise 8 (Page 124)
ACROSS: 1. jobs 3. architect 7. ill 8. teacher 9. pilots 12. is 13. secretary
16. seven 17. or 19. of 20. maids 2. mechanic 25. notes 27. part-time
28. want ads 30. travel agents 31. take
DOWN: 1. judge 2. butcher 3. aches 4. car 5. classified 6. lawyer 7. is
10 toy 11. artist 14. engineer 15. teams 16. son 18. change 19. on
21. do 23. truck 24. item 26. easel 27. poet 29. art

NTC ESL/EFL TEXTS AND MATERIAL
Junior High—Adult Education

Computer Software
Amigo
Basic Vocabulary Builder on Computer

Language and Culture Readers
Beginner's English Reader
Advanced Beginner's English Reader
Cultural Encounters in the U.S.A.
Passport to America Series
  California Discovery
  Adventures in the Southwest
  The Coast-to-Coast Mystery
  The New York Connection
Discover America Series
  California, Chicago, Florida, Hawaii,
  New England, New York, Texas,
  Washington, D.C.
Looking at America Series
  Looking at American Signs, Looking at
  American Food, Looking at American
  Recreation, Looking at American
  Holidays
Time: We the People
Communicative American English

Text/Audiocassette Learning Packages
Speak Up! Sing Out!
Listen and Say It Right in English!

Transparencies
Everyday Situations in English

**Duplicating Masters and
Black-line Masters**
The Complete ESL/EFL Cooperative and
  Communicative Activity Book
Easy Vocabulary Games
Vocabulary Games
Advanced Vocabulary Games
Play and Practice!
Basic Vocabulary Builder
Practical Vocabulary Builder
Beginning Activities for English
  Language Learners
Intermediate Activities for English
  Language Learners
Advanced Activities for English
  Language Learners

Language-Skills Texts
English with a Smile
English Survival Series
  Building Vocabulary, Recognizing
  Details, Identifying Main Ideas, Writing
  Sentences and Paragraphs, Using the
  Context
English Across the Curriculum
Essentials of Reading and Writing English
Everyday English
Learning to Listen in English
Listening to Communicate in English
Communication Skillbooks
Living in the U.S.A.
Basic Everyday Spelling Workbook
Practical Everyday Spelling Workbook
Advanced Readings and Communicative
  Activities for Oral Proficiency

Practical English Writing Skills
Express Yourself in Written English
Campus English
Speak English!
Read English!
Write English!
Orientation in American English
Building English Sentences
Grammar for Use
Grammar Step-by-Step
Listening by Doing
Reading by Doing
Speaking by Doing
Vocabulary by Doing
Writing by Doing
Look, Think and Write

Survival-Skills Texts
Building Real Life English Skills
Everyday Consumer English
Book of Forms
Essential Life Skills series
Finding a Job in the United States
English for Adult Living
Living in English
Prevocational English

TOEFL and University Preparation
NTC's Preparation Course for the
  TOEFL®
NTC's Practice Tests for the TOEFL®
How to Apply to American Colleges
  and Universities
The International Student's Guide
  to the American University

Dictionaries and References
ABC's of Languages and Linguistics
Everyday American English Dictionary
Building Dictionary Skills in
  English (workbook)
Beginner's Dictionary of American
  English Usage
Beginner's English Dictionary
  Workbook
NTC's American Idioms Dictionary
NTC's Dictionary of American Slang
  and Colloquial Expressions
NTC's Dictionary of Phrasal Verbs
NTC's Dictionary of Grammar
  Terminology
Essential American Idioms
Contemporary American Slang
Forbidden American English
101 American English Idioms
101 American English Proverbs
Idiom Workbook
Essentials of English Grammar
The Complete ESL/EFL Resource Book
Safari Grammar
Safari Punctuation
303 Dumb Spelling Mistakes
TESOL Professional Anthologies
  Grammar and Composition
  Listening, Speaking, and Reading
  Culture

For further information or a current catalog, write:
National Textbook Company
a division of *NTC Publishing Group*
4255 West Touhy Avenue
Lincolnwood, Illinois 60646-1975 U.S.A.